D0463258

STATE FLOWERS

★ ━━━━━━━━━━ ★

including the Commonwealth of Puerto Rico

Also by Elaine Landau

ALZHEIMER'S DISEASE
BLACK MARKET ADOPTION AND THE SALE OF
CHILDREN
THE CHEROKEES
COLIN POWELL: FOUR-STAR GENERAL
COWBOYS
DYSLEXIA
ENDANGERED PLANTS
INTERESTING INVERTEBRATES:
A LOOK AT SOME ANIMALS WITHOUT BACKBONES
JUPITER
LYME DISEASE
MARS
NAZI WAR CRIMINALS
NEPTUNE
ROBERT FULTON
SATURN
THE SIOUX
STATE BIRDS
INCLUDING THE COMMONWEALTH OF
PUERTO RICO
SURROGATE MOTHERS
TROPICAL RAIN FORESTS AROUND THE WORLD
WE HAVE AIDS
WE SURVIVED THE HOLOCAUST
WILDFLOWERS AROUND THE WORLD

OCT. 23 1992

STATE FLOWERS

INCLUDING THE COMMONWEALTH OF PUERTO RICO

★ ──────────── ★

BY ELAINE LANDAU

THIS BOOK IS THE PROPERTY OF
THE NATIONAL CITY PUBLIC LIBRARY
CHILDREN'S ROOM

FRANKLIN WATTS
NEW YORK ★ CHICAGO ★ LONDON ★ TORONTO ★ SYDNEY

★ ▬▬▬▬▬ ★

For the wonderful librarians
at state libraries throughout the country
who helped provide information for this book

Photographs copyright ©: Black Olive Studios: pp. 9, 18; Tom Ulrich: pp.
10, 36, 60; Root Resources: pp. 11 (Louise K. Broman), 20 (Mary A. Root),
41 (Kitty Kohout); Michigan Dept. of Natural Resources: pp. 12, 32;
California Dept. of Fish & Game: p. 13; Carlye Calvin: p. 14; Dennis Jones:
p. 15; Pennsylvania Game Commission: pp. 16, 48; Ricardo E. Allen/Delaware
Tourism Office: p. 17; Florida Dept. of Commerce, Division of Tourism: p.
19; Hawaii State Capitol, Office of Information: p. 21; Donald J. Leopold:
pp. 22, 23, 24, 25, 29, 31, 35, 39, 40, 45, 59; Kansas Wildlife & Parks: p.
26; U.S. Fish & Game Commission: pp. 27, 37; Louisiana Dept. of Agriculture
& Forestry: pp. 28, 34; Maryland Dept. of Natural Resources & Public
Affairs/Jayson Knott: p. 30; Minnesota Dept. of Natural Resources: p. 33; Coco
McCoy/Rainbow: pp. 38, 42; North Carolina Division of Travel & Tourism: pp.
43, 56; Craig Bihrle/North Dakota Game & Fish Dept.: p. 44; Oklahoma Dept.
of Wildlife Conservation: p. 46; Joe L. Barger/Leach Botanical Garden: p.
47; Rhode Island Tourism Division: p. 49; Horticultural Photography, Corvallis,
OR/Muriel Orans: p. 50; South Dakota Dept. of Tourism: p. 51; State of Tennessee:
p. 52; Dr. E.R. Degginger: p. 53; Utah Division of Wildlife Resources: p. 54;
Jerome Wexler/New England Stock Photo: p. 55; Pat & Tom Leeson/Photo
Researchers: p. 57; Dave Cruise/West Virginia Division of Tourism & Parks: p. 58.

Library of Congress Cataloging-in-Publication Data

Landau, Elaine.
State flowers / by Elaine Landau.
p.   cm.
Includes bibliographical references and index.
Summary: Describes each state's official flower and tells of
legends associated with the flower.
ISBN 0-531-20059-0
1. State flowers—United States—Juvenile literature.   [1. State
flowers.   2. Flowers.   3. Emblems, State.]   I. Title.   II. Series.
QK85.L36   1992
582.13′0973—dc20
92-8950 CIP AC

Copyright © 1992 by Elaine Landau
All rights reserved
Printed in the United States of America
6   5   4   3   2   1

CONTENTS

★ ■■■■■■■ ★

INTRODUCTION

★ ▰▰▰▰▰▰▰▰▰▰▰▰▰ ★

Throughout our nation's history, flowers have beautified America's landscapes. They grow in deserts, bogs, woodlands, and valleys as well as on mountains, plains, seacoasts, and other areas. Some are wildflowers that spring up on their own; others are grown in gardens. But whether they grow wild or in gardens, many flowers have such unusual shapes, brilliant colors, or pleasant fragrances that they are always a welcome sight.

Each state, as well as the District of Columbia and Puerto Rico, has adopted a state flower to represent it. Due to land development, overpicking, and other factors, some of these flowers are endangered. They were selected as state flowers to call attention to their plight and ensure that they don't become extinct. Other state flowers are so common throughout the state that legislators (lawmakers) felt that those flowers best represented the area. A number of state flowers played an important role in their state's history. Often these blossoms proved useful to American Indians or early pioneers in some way.

While many states have kept the first state flower they adopted, others have passed new laws to change their choice. Some states have even had several state flowers over the years. A number of states have kept detailed records of how they chose their flower or flowers. Others have little information about such choices. Nevertheless, wherever possible, this book tries to show you how and why state flowers were selected.

It's interesting to see which flowers were selected by the various states. Together, these blossoms form a rich and colorful carpet reflecting our national heritage.

Note: In this book, the state flowers are described state by state and the states are arranged in alphabetical order. Two names are given for every flower. The first is its common name, the one most people use to identify the flower. The second name, the one in brackets, is the name scientists use.

▰▰▰▰▰▰▰▰▰▰▰

ALABAMA

Camellia [*Camellia japonica*]

The camellia is a semitropical Asian shrub that bears showy red, white, pink, or colorfully speckled blossoms. The camellia's flower petals tend to be heavy and waxy, while its dark-green leaves are shiny. Camellia blossoms look very much like roses. Because of their beauty, these flowers are often used in corsages.

The camellia wasn't always Alabama's state flower. It was officially adopted by the state legislature on August 26, 1959. But for over thirty years before that the goldenrod was Alabama's state flower. Alabama schoolchildren chose the goldenrod when asked to pick their favorite blossom. While the goldenrod is a bright and pleasant flower, some people feel that the groves of camellias growing in Alabama are splendid.

ALASKA

★ ▬▬▬▬ ★

Forget-Me-Not [*Myosotis alpestris*]

The forget-me-not is a small blue flower with a bright-yellow center. These dainty blossoms often grow in long clusters curved at the tip.

There are a number of legends about the forget-me-not. According to one story, a young man drowned trying to swim across a river to gather these flowers for his love. Just before going under, he yelled, "Forget me not!" to the horrified girl, who watched from the riverbank.

The forget-me-not was officially adopted as Alaska's state flower on April 28, 1917. It was thought to be a good choice since this wildflower can be found throughout the vast state. The forget-me-not's faithful appearance each year also reminded Alaskans of their early pioneers' enduring spirit. These settlers overcame tremendous hardships to live in a wild and beautiful land whose state motto is "North to the Future."

▬▬▬

ARIZONA

Saguaro, or Giant Cactus *[Cereus giganteus]*

The saguaro, or giant cactus, is a huge Southwestern plant that may grow up to 60 feet (18 m) high and weigh many tons. It is slow-growing, often gaining no more than 6 inches (15 cm) in the first ten years of its life. This cactus bears waxy greenish-white funnel-shaped blossoms. The flowers are usually between 3 and 4 inches (8–10 cm) long. Although these blossoms bloom at night, they generally remain open for most of the following day. While open, they are visited by flower bats, insects, and birds.

Before Arizona became a state, its territorial legislature adopted the saguaro as the area's official flower on March 18, 1901. When the territory became a state, it kept the saguaro, and it remains Arizona's state flower today. The Indian paintbrush (Wyoming's state flower) had also been considered as a choice for Arizona's state flower. But it was argued that the saguaro was better suited for this honor since the Indian paintbrush is a parasitic plant (it lives off other vegetation). In addition, the saguaro is an easily seen, unique plant of the Sonoran Desert in the southern part of the state.

ARKANSAS

Apple Blossom *[Pyrus malus]*

The apple blossom is an attractive, dainty white flower that blooms on apple trees in the spring. The blossoms are in the rose family and in fact look like tiny roses.

Arkansas' General Assembly adopted the apple blossom as its state flower on January 30, 1901. Not very much is known about why it was chosen. Unlike some other states, Arkansas did not save these early documents.

The apple blossom is also Michigan's state flower. For more information, look under *Michigan*.

CALIFORNIA

★ ■■■■■■■■■■■■■ ★

California Poppy, or Golden Poppy *[Eschscholtzia californica]*

The California, or golden, poppy is a four-petaled funnel-shaped flower. This deep-golden blossom blooms from February to September. California poppies are found over much of the state's grasslands as well as in other parts of California.

During California's early history, sailors on passing ships thought the brightly colored flowers looked like glowing gold blankets spread across the rolling hills. That's why they nicknamed the region "Land of Fire." Although today the blossom is most commonly known as the California poppy, it is sometimes also called the golden poppy or the flame flower.

In 1890, the California State Floral Society suggested that the California poppy would make an excellent state flower. It was officially adopted by California's state legislature on March 2, 1903.

COLORADO

★ ▬▬▬▬▬ ★

Rocky Mountain Columbine *[Aquilegia caerules]*

The Rocky Mountain columbine is a magnificent white and lavender-blue flower with a yellow center. It usually blooms between June and August and is frequently found in abundance on cliffs and rocky slopes.

Colorado schoolchildren picked the Rocky Mountain columbine as their choice for state flower over fifty other blossoms. Runners-up included the mariposa lily, yucca, wild rose, and goldenrod.

The Rocky Mountain columbine was adopted as the state flower on April 4, 1899. Its brilliant colors were thought to represent the state—blue for Colorado skies, white for its snows, and yellow for Colorado gold.

COMMONWEALTH OF PUERTO RICO

★ ▬▬▬▬▬▬▬ ★

Maga *[Thespesia grandiflora]*

The maga is an evergreen tree that grows from 30 to 50 feet (9–15 m) high. It bears large, five-petaled red flowers. The maga is frequently found in the moist limestone forest regions of Puerto Rico.

In 1980 the Puerto Rican legislature proposed making the maga Puerto Rico's national flower. Although this bill was never voted on, the maga is generally regarded as the island's official flower.

CONNECTICUT

Mountain Laurel [*Kalmia latifolia*]

The mountain laurel is an evergreen plant in the heath family that grows to the height of a shrub or small tree. It bears fragrant pink and white blossoms that sometimes have purple markings.

The mountain laurel was adopted as Connecticut's state flower on April 17, 1907. It was chosen because its striking beauty had caught the eye of travelers since colonial times. In Connecticut, the flowers tend to bloom near the end of June, brightening the state's forests and fields. Sometimes the mountain laurel is also called the calico bush and the spoonwood.

The mountain laurel is Pennsylvania's state flower too. For more information, look under *Pennsylvania*.

DELAWARE

★ ▬▬▬▬▬ ★

Peach Blossom [*Prunus persica*]

The peach blossom is a pink flower seen on peach trees in the spring. These flowers bloom on the tree even before the tree's leaves appear. At times, the delicate blossoms are damaged by a late frost.

The peach blossom was officially adopted by Delaware's legislature on May 9, 1985, because of Delaware's large peach-growing industry. At the time the peach blossom became the state flower, over 800,000 peach trees grew in Delaware and the area was called the "Peach State."

DISTRICT OF COLUMBIA

★ ▬▬▬▬▬▬▬▬▬▬▬ ★

American Beauty Rose [*Rosa*]

The rose is considered one of the world's loveliest and most popular flowers. In 1986, it was officially adopted as the United States' national flower.

There are many kinds of roses. These blossoms exist in a wide range of types and colors. Some roses grow wild, while others are cultivated, or grown, in greenhouses and gardens. The cultivated roses generally have double blossoms—this means that the flower's petals are arranged in several layers.

There are pink, yellow, red, and white roses. Botanists have even developed several types of lavender roses. Among the most popular roses are some of the hybrids. A hybrid rose is a flower bred from two separate varieties of roses.

The American Beauty rose was adopted as the official flower of the District of Columbia on June 6, 1925. This rose is a hybrid that is well known for its wonderfully fragrant flowers. Although at one time American Beauty roses were in great demand, they are no longer commercially grown by major flower producers.

The rose is also *New York*'s state flower. For more information, look under that state.

FLORIDA

Orange Blossom [*Citrus sinensis*]

The orange blossom is a sweet-smelling white flower that blooms on orange trees. After the flowers appear, some of these blossoms develop into oranges. These fruits are high in vitamin C and are enjoyed by people in various areas of the world.

The orange blossom was made Florida's official state flower in the spring of 1909. The exact date of its adoption was not recorded. The orange blossom was selected for two reasons: it represents Florida's large orange industry and is commonly found throughout the state.

GEORGIA

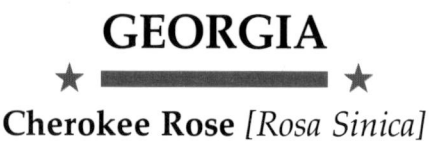

Cherokee Rose *[Rosa Sinica]*

The Cherokee rose is a waxy white flower that blooms on a thorny climbing shrub. The blossom has a large yellow center and petals that feel like velvet. This rose is named for the Cherokee Indians, who once actively spread the plant throughout the area. It originally came from China.

These attractive flowers bloom each year in early spring. If weather conditions are favorable, Cherokee roses may flower a second time in the fall.

At the suggestion of the Georgia Federation of Women's Clubs, Georgia officially adopted the Cherokee rose as its state flower on August 18, 1916.

HAWAII

Native Yellow Hibiscus [*Hibiscus brackenridgei A. Gray*]

The native yellow hibiscus, a shrub, bears beautiful large yellow blossoms that are deep red at the base. It's one of numerous colorful hibiscus flowers found in Hawaii. Many of these blossoms have been used by Hawaiians for decoration as well as to make medicines and dyes.

In 1923, the legislature of what was then the territory of Hawaii adopted the hibiscus as its official flower. At the time, no particular flower color was mentioned. The flower's color was determined on June 6, 1988, when the state of Hawaii chose the native yellow hibiscus.

Unaware of the 1988 law, the Hawaiian Telephone Company mistakenly cited the red hibiscus as the state flower in its 1989 directory. Following the error, a four-day telephone poll was conducted to determine which flower the public preferred. Residents were invited to call in to vote for their favorite-color hibiscus. The red hibiscus received 20,386 votes; the yellow hibiscus only 4,330. Of course, this was only a poll, not a real election, and less than 25,000 people participated. (The population of Hawaii is about 1 million). So, the beautiful yellow blossom remains Hawaii's official state flower.

IDAHO

Syringa [*Philadelphus lewisii*]

The syringa is a shrub with short leafy branches. It bears clusters of white, sweet-smelling, four-petaled flowers.

These flowers were first noted by Captain Meriwether Lewis of the Lewis and Clark expedition to the Pacific Northwest in 1805–1806. The flower's scientific name, *Philadelphus lewisii*, honors Captain Lewis. (The first word, *Philadelphus*, is Latin for "brotherly.")

Idaho became a state in 1890, and three years later the syringa unofficially became its state flower. The Idaho legislature made it the state's official choice on March 2, 1931.

ILLINOIS

Native Violet [*Viola sororio*]

There are many kinds of violets in many different environments. Often the leaves are heart-shaped, but there are violets with lobed and long, narrow leaves. Although some types of violets have creamy white, pink, or yellow flowers, the most popular ones bear deep-blue or violet five-petaled blossoms.

The violet is the state flower of Illinois. When Illinois schoolchildren cast their ballots to select a state flower, the violet received the most votes. The native violet was officially adopted as the state flower on February 21, 1908.

The violet is also the state flower of *New Jersey*, *Rhode Island*, and *Wisconsin*.

INDIANA

Peony [*Paeonia*]

Peonies are a group of plants in the buttercup family that bear large, showy, single- or double-blossomed flowers. These flowers may be white, red, or rose-colored. Peonies, which usually bloom toward the end of May and in early June, are widely grown throughout the state. They are often used to decorate the graves of soldiers on Memorial Day.

Indiana has actually had four state flowers since 1913. The peony is the latest, and its supporters hope it will be the last. The others were the carnation (adopted in 1913), the tulip tree blossom (adopted in 1923), and the common zinnia (adopted in 1931). During the 1950s, a movement began to select a state flower commonly grown within the state. Among the peony's strongest supporters was an Indiana legislator who also happened to make his living growing peonies. With his help, on March 13, 1957, the peony was adopted as Indiana's newest state flower.

IOWA

★ ▬▬▬ ★

Wild Rose [*Rosa pratincola*,
scientific name for Wild Prairie Rose]

The wild rose is a large, showy pink blossom with a yellow center. These flowers grow on curved stems and have saw-tooth-edged leaves. They bloom from June through late summer.

The wild rose was adopted as Iowa's state flower on May 7, 1897. These big colorful blossoms were admired by both young and old Iowa residents. Although Iowa legislators didn't mention a particular species (type) of wild rose, the wild prairie rose is usually given the honor.

The wild prairie rose is also *North Dakota*'s state flower.

KANSAS

Native Sunflower [*Helianthus annuus*]

The sunflower is a plant that grows between 3 and 10 feet (1–3 m) tall. It has showy yellow flower heads that may measure over a foot (0.3 m) wide. The many flowers of the central disk are bordered by a fringe of larger yellow petals. During the day, sunflowers turn toward the sun.

Kansas, which is often called the "Sunflower State," adopted the wild native sunflower as its state flower on March 12, 1903. The sunflower was selected because the plant is hardy, is found throughout much of Kansas, and is thought to represent the state's glorious frontier prairie days. The legislative act adopting the sunflower declares that it "has to all Kansans a historic symbolism which speaks of frontier days, winding trails, pathless prairies, and is full of the life and glory of the past. . . ."

KENTUCKY

Goldenrod [*Solidago altissima*]

Goldenrod is a wildflower that grows in clusters toward the top of its thin rodlike stem. As the name suggests, these flowers are usually brilliant yellow or deep-gold in color. The goldenrod is so bright and attractive that two states, Kentucky and *Nebraska*, have adopted it. And some floral societies think it should be our national flower.

Before the goldenrod's selection, many Kentucky residents thought of the bluegrass blossom as their unofficial state flower. The United States War Department even chose it as a symbol for Kentucky's militia.

However, the State Federation of Women's Clubs wanted the goldenrod to represent Kentucky. Although the War Department argued for the bluegrass blossom, Kentucky's state legislature received numerous petitions urging it to adopt the goldenrod instead. The legislature listened to the voters' voices, and on March 26, 1926, it made the goldenrod Kentucky's state flower. Since then, the goldenrod's status as state flower has been unsuccessfully challenged several times by supporters of the dogwood blossom and the redbud.

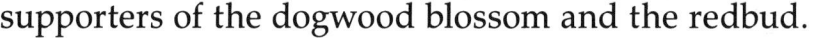

LOUISIANA

★ ▬▬▬▬▬▬▬▬ ★

Magnolia [*Magnolia grandiflora*]

On August 1, 1900, the magnolia became Louisiana's state flower. In the 1950s, the Louisiana Iris Society tried to have the state flower changed to the blue iris because it grows primarily in Louisiana while the magnolia grows in much of the South.

But magnolia defenders stressed that the blue iris is often found in unattractive swamp areas and is a less hardy flower than the magnolia blossom. They also pointed out that Louisiana's state capitol building is trimmed with numerous bronze magnolias.

When the legislature voted on the issue, the magnolia triumphed. It has continued as Louisiana's state flower ever since. It is also *Mississippi's* state flower.

MAINE

★ ▬▬▬ ★

White Pine Cone and Tassel *[Pinus strobus]*

The long slender pine cone and tassel found on the eastern white pine tree is Maine's state flower. Eastern white pines are huge trees that may grow to a height of 100 feet (30 m). They are common throughout New England and are highly valued for their smooth light-colored lumber.

During November and December of 1894, the Maine Floral Emblem Society held a contest to select a state flower. Ballots were published in newspapers throughout the state, and everyone was urged to vote. The pine cone and tassel was the popular choice. It was adopted as Maine's state flower on February 1, 1925.

MARYLAND

★ ▬▬▬▬▬▬▬ ★

Black-eyed Susan [*Rudbeckia hirta*]

The black-eyed Susan is a small wildflower with a dark cone-shaped cluster of many tiny flowers called florets at the center and a fringe of larger golden-orange petals. Each flower head grows on a single stem. The leaves of the black-eyed Susan are stiff and hairy.

Black-eyed Susans usually bloom between May and October. These flowers are frequently seen growing in fields and along roadsides, where they provide a bright splash of color and food for wildlife. The black-eyed Susan was adopted as Maryland's state flower on April 18, 1918.

MASSACHUSETTS

★ ━━━━━━━ ★

Mayflower, or Trailing Arbutus [Epigaea repens]

The mayflower is a slow-growing evergreen trailing plant that bears white or pink flowers. Its five-petaled blossoms are both fragrant and pleasing to look at. Although in other parts of the country this plant is usually called the trailing arbutus, it is known as the mayflower in New England. Some people think it may have been named after the ship that brought the Pilgrims to Plymouth, Massachusetts.

Massachusetts legislators chose the mayflower as the state flower over the water lily and the lilac. It was officially adopted on May 1, 1918. It is presently illegal in Massachusetts to dig up or in any way injure a mayflower growing on public property. Digging and trampling have eliminated this plant from many areas.

MICHIGAN

★ ▬▬▬▬▬ ★

Apple Blossom [*Pyrus coronaria*]

The apple blossom became Michigan's state flower on April 28, 1897. It was chosen to represent the state because blooming apple trees add beauty and brightness to Michigan's countryside.

Michigan apples are well known throughout the world for their delicious taste. The state has been among the nation's leading apple producers since the nineteenth century. It is likely that Michigan's first apple tree seeds were brought to the area by American Indians. However, according to legend, at least a few Michigan apple trees sprang from seeds planted by Johnny Chapman, popularly known as "Johnny Appleseed." Johnny Appleseed, a famous pioneer folk hero, traveled throughout America planting apple seeds.

The apple blossom is described under *Arkansas*.

▬▬▬▬▬

MINNESOTA

★ ━━━━━━━━ ★

Pink and White Lady's Slipper [*Cypripedium reginae*]

The pink and white lady's slipper is a beautiful, slow-growing white flower with one enlarged bright-pink petal. This colorful petal forms the blossom's "lip" and shapes the flower to look something like a shoe. That's why it is named the lady's slipper and is sometimes called a moccasin flower. Swamps and other wet areas are favored by pink and white lady's slippers. They are in the orchid family and are related to the exotic orchids that grow wild in the tropics or are cultivated in greenhouses.

On February 19, 1902, the Minnesota state legislature adopted the pink and white lady's slipper as the state flower. Minnesota also took measures to protect this special blossom. On April 25, 1925, a law was passed stating that "no person within the state of Minnesota shall knowingly buy (or) sell the state flower." The law also prohibits taking these flowers from public lands.

MISSISSIPPI

Magnolia [*Magnolia grandiflora*]

In 1900, Mississippi schoolchildren voted to select a state flower. The magnolia received the most votes. Over a half century later, on February 26, 1952, Mississippi officially adopted the magnolia as its state flower. And the magnolia tree, on which the flower blooms, was selected as Mississippi's state tree.

The magnolia is also *Louisiana*'s state flower.

MISSOURI

★ ━━━━━ ★

Hawthorn (the white hawthorn blossom) *[Crataegus]*

The hawthorn is a thorny shrub or small tree that bears white blossoms. These attractive flowers grow in clusters and usually bloom during April and May. The flowers are followed by small, applelike fruit.

The hawthorn was thought to be a good choice to represent Missouri. Its scientific name, *Crataegus*, means "strength" in Greek—a quality that many Missourians feel describes their state. In addition, the flower's white color was thought to stand for the state's pure ideals.

The white blossom was officially adopted as Missouri's state flower on March 16, 1923. Hawthorns grow in large numbers throughout Missouri.

MONTANA

Bitterroot [*Lewisia rediviva*]

The bitterroot is a pink blossom that grows close to the ground. Its scientific name, *Lewisia rediviva*, honors Meriwether Lewis of the Lewis and Clark expedition. In 1805, these explorers noted the delicate flower in a western Montana valley.

The bitterroot has long been recognized as being both attractive and practical. Years ago the flower's root was an important part of the American Indians' diet. The Indians dug out the root and cleaned and cooked it. Sometimes it was mixed with berries or meat. These roots were also a valuable trading item. At some trading posts, a large sack of the roots might even be exchanged for a horse.

In 1894, Montana residents voted to choose a state flower. A total of 5,857 ballots was cast for thirty-two different flowers. Receiving 3,621 votes, the bitterroot was the winner. On March 19, 1895, Montana's state legislature officially adopted it as the state flower.

NEBRASKA

★ ▬▬▬▬▬ ★

Goldenrod *[Solidago gigantea]*

The goldenrod was adopted as Nebraska's state flower on April 4, 1985, for two reasons: it has a long growing season, and its hardiness symbolizes the Nebraska pioneers' strength. The goldenrod is described under *Kentucky*.

NEVADA

Sagebrush [*Artemisia tridentata*]

Sagebrush is a branching bush found throughout much of Nevada. Known for its sweet smell, this straight-stemmed grayish-green plant may grow from 1 to 12 feet (0.3–3.7 m) tall. Sagebrush bears yellow blossoms that are actually made up of florets.

This flowering bush grows in dry desert and mountain regions where many other plants are unable to survive. Frequently, it is used as food for sheep and cattle during the winter months, and is the primary food of pronghorn antelope, mule deer, and sage grouse.

Years ago, American Indians relied on sagebrush to fuel their fires. They also made tea from the plant. Early Nevada pioneers frequently settled where the sagebrush grew high because they believed the land was most fertile there. Since those early days, Nevada has been nicknamed the "Sagebrush State." Sagebrush officially became Nevada's state flower in 1917.

NEW HAMPSHIRE

★ ▬▬▬▬▬▬▬▬▬▬▬ ★

Purple Lilac [Syringa vulgaris]

The purple lilac is a bush with spreading branches that bears clusters of lavender flowers. These blossoms are often admired for their wonderful color and fragrance.

The selection of the purple lilac as New Hampshire's state flower grew out of a heated debate in the state's legislature. Nine other flowers had been suggested for this honor. Among these were the apple blossom, purple aster, goldenrod, and the water lily. However, the purple lilac was the most popular. It was officially adopted as New Hampshire's state flower on March 28, 1919.

Rochester, New Hampshire, is often called the "Lilac City." Over half a century ago, William H. Champlin, a Rochester resident, planted hundreds of lilac bushes along a mile of roadway leading to his home. His efforts to beautify the city led to numerous lilac plantings throughout the area.

NEW JERSEY

Native Violet [*Viola sororio*]

The native violet became New Jersey's state flower in 1913. There the flower had been especially admired for its beautiful deep-blue color. Violets are commonly found throughout the state.

The violet is described under *Illinois*.

NEW MEXICO

Yucca [*Yucca elata*]

Although a number of different yucca plants may be found in New Mexico, the one chosen as the official state flower grows nearly as tall as a tree. In the summer, this yucca bears cream-colored blossoms. These bell-shaped flowers grow in clusters along stems that jut out from groups of pointed leaves.

The yucca flowers are sometimes called "*Los Candelarios de Dios*," which means "the Candles of God" in Spanish. According to one legend, missionaries who first came to New Mexico were taken aback by the sight of the blooming yucca in the scorched desert. It is said that the missionaries piously dropped to their knees to pray among these candles of God. The yucca plant had practical uses too. Both Southwestern Indians and settlers used its roots to make soap and its leaves and stems to fashion mats. The tender young flower stalks were eaten.

Schoolchildren in New Mexico were asked to pick a state flower. After months of discussing different blossoms, they overwhelmingly voted for the yucca. On March 14, 1927, New Mexico's state legislature officially made the yucca the state flower.

NEW YORK

Rose [*Rosa*]

On Arbor Day in 1891, New York state's schoolchildren picked the wild rose in a poll taken at their schools. Their second choice had been the goldenrod. The wild rose was adopted as New York's state flower on April 20, 1955. No particular color of wild rose was mentioned in the legislation passed.

NORTH CAROLINA

Dogwood [Cornus florida]

The dogwood is a shrub or small tree with spreading branches. What we usually think of as the dogwood's petals are actually large showy modified leaves that surround the tree's small greenish-white flowers. Although these attractive "false petals" are usually white, they may sometimes be pink or even a deep rose color in cultivated varieties.

In the 1930s, a bill to make the oxeye daisy North Carolina's state flower was defeated. Later, on March 15, 1941, the dogwood was adopted as the state flower. The dogwood was chosen for its beauty and because it is found throughout the state.

The dogwood is also *Virginia*'s state flower.

NORTH DAKOTA

★ ━━━━━━━━ ★

Wild Prairie Rose [*Rosa pratincola*]

North Dakota's state flower is the wild prairie rose. The blossom first served as a symbol for the state as far back as 1891. At that time, the State University of North Dakota picked pink and green—the colors of the wild prairie rose—for its school colors. When North Dakota schoolchildren were asked to vote for a state flower, they chose the wild prairie rose. It was adopted as the state flower on March 7, 1907.

The wild rose is described under *Iowa*.

OHIO

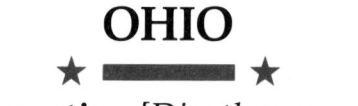

Scarlet Carnation [*Dianthus caryophyllus*]

The scarlet carnation is a showy, fragrant red flower. These hardy and popular blossoms were first brought to the United States from southern Europe. Today they are grown both outdoors and in greenhouses.

On February 3, 1904, the scarlet carnation was made Ohio's state flower in memory of William McKinley, our twenty-fifth president. McKinley was born in the small rural town of Niles, Ohio. The scarlet carnation had been the president's favorite flower. He always wore one on his jacket lapel.

In 1901, at the start of his second presidential term, William McKinley was killed by an assassin. Even after being struck by the bullet, the dying president had called out to the angry crowd not to harm the man who had shot him. Reflecting the president's spirit, the bill later adopted by Ohio's General Assembly read: ". . . May the scarlet carnation as our state flower . . . represent the good that is within us."

OKLAHOMA

★ ▬▬▬▬▬▬ ★

Mistletoe [*Phoradendron flavescens*]

Mistletoe is an evergreen plant that bears tiny yellow flowers. In addition to its blossoms, the mistletoe also produces small white berries. Mistletoe is frequently found growing on the trunks and branches of trees. It is a parasitic plant. This means that it lives off other vegetation instead of manufacturing its own food.

The mistletoe was adopted as Oklahoma's official flower on February 11, 1893, before the territory became a state. Among the stories of how it was chosen is the tale of a young New York attorney and his bride, who were among the territory's early settlers. When the woman was expecting the couple's first child, she became quite ill and was advised to return East for care. However, she refused to go without her husband, who felt unable to leave at the time. Both the mother and infant died during childbirth. As it was close to Christmas and there were no fresh flowers for their grave, friends placed mistletoe on the coffin that held both the mother and child. Supposedly, following the funeral, family friends in the legislature introduced a bill to make the mistletoe Oklahoma's official flower.

Although there may be more than one account of how Oklahoma chose the mistletoe, Oklahoma was, nevertheless, the first territory or state to adopt an official flower.

▬▬▬▬▬▬

OREGON

★ ▬▬▬▬ ★

Oregon Grape [*Berberis aquifolium*]

The Oregon grape is a low-lying shrub that bears clusters of small, six-petaled, bright-yellow flowers. The Oregon grape is in the barberry family and not really a grape. The plant produces sour berries, which are frequently eaten by bears. People use the berries for food too, by adding sweetener and making jelly or a beverage from them. The shrub's leaves look especially attractive in the fall when they turn bright red.

The Oregon grape was adopted as Oregon's state flower on January 31, 1899.

▬▬▬▬

PENNSYLVANIA

Mountain Laurel [*Kalmia latifolia*]

In 1933, problems arose when Pennsylvania's Senate decided to choose a state flower. The lawmakers passed two bills—each selecting a different flower to represent the state. It was then up to Governor Gifford Pinchot to decide whether the mountain laurel or the wild honeysuckle would be Pennsylvania's official flower. It is rumored that the governor left the choice up to his wife, who picked the mountain laurel. On May 5, 1933, it was officially adopted as the state flower.

The mountain laurel is commonly found in Pennsylvania's mountains, where it usually blooms by mid-June. Every year a laurel festival is held in Tioga County, Pennsylvania, near the Leonard Harrison State Park. The annual celebration draws hundreds of people who come to admire these beautiful flowers.

The mountain laurel is described under *Connecticut*.

RHODE ISLAND

★ ▬▬▬▬▬▬▬▬▬ ★

Early Blue Violet [*Viola palmata*]

When Rhode Island schoolchildren were given the task of selecting their state's flower, they chose the violet. Sometimes called the early blue violet, the species (type) chosen by Rhode Island usually blooms between April and May. It was officially adopted as the state flower on March 11, 1968.

The violet is described under *Illinois*.

SOUTH CAROLINA

★ ▬▬▬▬▬▬▬▬▬▬▬▬ ★

Yellow Jessamine [*Gelseminum sempervirens*]

The yellow jessamine is a delicate trumpet-shaped flower that blooms on a climbing vine. It frequently grows on trees, fences, and fields in South Carolina. This golden blossom is known for its wonderful fragrance.

In 1923 South Carolina's state legislature appointed a committee to pick a flower to represent their state. By February 1, 1924, the yellow jessamine was adopted as South Carolina's state flower. Several reasons were given for its selection: it is widely found throughout much of the state, its bright color reminded some people of the purity of gold, and its faithful appearance each spring was thought to suggest patriotism and loyalty to the state.

SOUTH DAKOTA

★ ▬▬▬▬▬▬▬▬▬▬ ★

American Pasqueflower [*Anemone patens*]

The American pasqueflower is a small lavender blossom covered with silky white hairs. These flowers grow wild in many parts of South Dakota and usually bloom between March and June. The American pasqueflower's yearly appearance throughout much of the state is often considered one of the first signs of spring.

The blossom is sometimes also called the windflower. Its scientific name—*Anemone*—comes from the Greek word meaning "wind." The American pasqueflower was adopted as South Dakota's state flower on March 5, 1903.

TENNESSEE

Iris *[Iridaceae]*

The iris is a large, colorful flower often found growing in swampy wetland areas. There are about 170 different species, or types, of irises. These flowers span a broad range of colors. Some are gold, orange, and black, while others combine shades of purple and lavender. The name "iris" comes from a Greek word meaning "colors of the rainbow."

On April 22, 1933, Tennessee adopted the iris as its state flower. The bill passed by the Tennessee legislature did not specify a particular iris, but the purple iris is usually considered the state flower.

TEXAS

★ ▬▬▬▬▬ ★

Bluebonnet *[Lupinus subcarnosus; Lupinus texensis; Lupinus havardii; Lupinus concinnus; Lupinus plattensis]*

The bluebonnet is a deep-blue, five-petaled flower shaped something like a woman's sunbonnet.

There are many tales concerning this wildflower. According to one Indian legend, a terrible storm once covered the land with water. The flood was followed by an extended drought, which in turn was followed by a freezing winter. Before long, all the plants and wildlife had died. The starving Indians prayed to the Great Spirit for help.

The Great Spirit asked the tribe to burn its most precious possession and throw the ashes to the wind. One young Indian girl especially wanted to help her people. So late that night she secretly burned a doll which she loved more than any of her other things and tossed its ashes to the wind. The doll had had a blue-feathered headdress. The next morning the barren land was covered with lovely blue blossoms that matched the color of the doll's outfit. A time of plenty had returned for the tribe.

Texas actually has five state flowers—five different types of bluebonnets. On March 7, 1901, the Texas legislature had selected one species of the bluebonnet, *Lupinus subcarnosus*, as its state flower. However, in 1971, this act was amended to include all types of bluebonnet flowers.

▬▬▬▬▬

UTAH

★ ▬▬▬ ★

Sego Lily [*Calochortus nuttalli*]

The sego lily is a fragrant, satiny, white tulip-shaped blossom. The flower's base is yellow with purplish markings. The sego lily has a slender stem and narrow leaves.

This small flower actually played a large role in helping Utah's early pioneers to survive. In the spring of 1848, settlers had been struck by misfortune. First, the grain crops they had planted were attacked by swarms of crickets. Later on, drought and frost worsened the damage.

Fortunately, friendly Indians told the settlers that the bulb of the sego lily was both delicious and healthful. They taught the pioneers how to dig out the flowers' bulbs and prepare them as food. Before long, word of the edible bulb spread, and hundreds of pioneers were saved from starvation.

As time passed, hunting for wild sego lily bulbs became a popular pioneer custom among children. They delighted their parents as they returned home with buckets filled with these sweet-tasting bulbs. When Utah schoolchildren were asked to choose a state flower, the sego lily received the most votes. On March 18, 1911, the Utah legislature passed a bill that officially made it the state's flower.

VERMONT

★ ▬▬▬▬▬ ★

Red Clover [*Trifolium pratense*]

Red clover is a small plant that produces purplish-red flowers in round clusters. These clovers have three small palm-shaped leaves, or leaflets. Some people believe that if you find a four-leaf clover, good luck will come to you.

Red clover grows wild and also is cultivated as a crop. These crops are often grown as food for farm animals. Red clover is frequently planted to enrich the soil for various other important farm crops. Growing clover adds extra nitrogen to the earth, which enables crops to do especially well.

In early America, pioneers dried these flower heads to make a healing tea. Although today red clover is a common sight in Vermont fields and along its roadsides, the flower is not native to the state. It was brought over from Europe. On February 1, 1894, red clover was adopted as Vermont's state flower.

VIRGINIA

Dogwood *[Cornus florida]*

The Garden Club of Virginia actively campaigned for the dogwood's selection as Virginia's state flower. Its efforts proved successful when on March 6, 1918, the dogwood was adopted by the state legislature. In 1932, the Garden Club began a project to further encourage dogwood planting in Virginia. The project's slogan was "A million dogwoods by 1935."

The dogwood is described under *North Carolina.*

WASHINGTON

★ ■■■■■■■■■ ★

Coast Rhododendron [*Rhododendron macrophyllum*]

The coast rhododendron is an evergreen shrub that usually grows to between 4 and 12 feet (1.2–3.7 m) tall. This shrub bears beautiful bell-shaped blossoms that are pink and deep rose in color.

In Washington, six different blossoms were considered for the state flower. However, before long, the choice was narrowed down to two—the coast rhododendron and the clover. Following a heated debate among supporters of both flowers, the issue was put to a vote. When the ballots were counted, the coast rhododendron received 7,704 votes while the clover had only 5,720. Since a group of Washington women had been among the flower's strongest supporters, the coast rhododendron became known as "the ladies' choice." On January 19, 1949, the state legislature officially made it Washington's state flower.

Another type of rhododendron, known as the big laurel, is *West Virginia*'s state flower.

WEST VIRGINIA

★ ▬▬▬▬▬▬▬▬▬ ★

Rhododendron, or Big Laurel [*Rhododendron maximum*]

The rhododendron, often called the big laurel, is an evergreen shrub that bears pale-pink or white blossoms. The flowers may also be dotted with tiny specks of red or yellow. West Virginia schoolchildren selected the rhododendron as the state flower, and it was officially adopted on January 23, 1903.

The coast rhododendron, *Washington*'s state flower, is related to the rhododendron.

WISCONSIN

★ ━━━━━━━━━━ ★

Wood Violet [*Viola papilionacea*]

The violet proved to be the favorite flower of Wisconsin schoolchildren. In a statewide contest, it received more votes than the wild rose, the trailing arbutus, and the white water lily. The wood violet was officially made Wisconsin's state flower in 1908. It is frequently found in wooded areas and on limestone ledges.

The violet is described under *Illinois*.

WYOMING

★ ▬▬▬▬▬▬▬ ★

Indian Paintbrush *[Castilleja linariaefolia]*

The Indian paintbrush is a plant with a slender stem and narrow, green bottom leaves. Toward the stem's top, the leaves become broader and bright red in color. These wide red leaves are called bracts and look very much like flower petals. Although the plant actually has tiny green blossoms, the brightly colored bracts are generally thought of as the plant's flower.

The Indian paintbrush was selected as Wyoming's state flower because it can be found nearly everywhere in the state. It was adopted on January 31, 1917. A specially commissioned picture of the flower was then hung in the state's Historical Department.

▬▬▬▬▬

GLOSSARY

★ ▬▬▬▬▬ ★

bract—a type of leaf that sometimes looks as if it is part of a flower

cultivate—to plant and tend

evergreen—a plant or tree that has leaves throughout the year

greenhouse—a building made largely of glass in which plants are grown and protected

hybrid—the offspring of two different plant types

leaflet—part of a compound leaf

parasitic plant—a plant that does not manufacture all its own food, but lives off other vegetation

semitropical—a warm steamy area similar to the tropics

shrub—a low-standing woody plant with several stems

species—a kind or type of plant with certain characteristics in common

speckled—marked with specks of another shade or color

▬▬▬▬

FOR FURTHER READING

Borland, Hal. *Plants of Christmas.* New York: Crowell, 1987.

Busch, Phyllis. *Wildflowers and the Stories Behind Their Names.* New York: Scribner, 1977.

Coil, Suzanne M. *Poisonous Plants.* New York: Franklin Watts, 1991.

Dowden, Anne Ophelia. *The Clover and the Bee: A Book of Pollination.* New York: Crowell, 1990.

———. *From Flower to Fruit.* New York: Crowell, 1984.

Landau, Elaine. *Endangered Plants.* New York: Franklin Watts, 1991.

Lauber, Patricia. *From Flower to Flower: Animals and Pollination.* New York: Crown, 1986.

Lerner, Carol. *Moonseed and Mistletoe: A Book of Poisonous Plants.* New York: Morrow, 1988.

Parker, Philip. *Life Cycle of a Sunflower.* New York: Franklin Watts (Bookwright), 1988.

Podendorf, Illa. *Weeds and Wildflowers.* Chicago: Childrens Press, 1981.

Selsam, Millicent. *Tree Flowers.* New York: Morrow, 1984.

Wexler, Jerome. *Flowers, Fruits, and Seeds.* Englewood Cliffs, N.J.: Prentice Hall, 1987.

Wiggers, Raymond. *Picture Guide to Tree Leaves.* New York: Franklin Watts, 1991.

INDEX

★ ▬▬▬ ★